J.M. EDISON

GRILL AND BARBECUE

The Ultimate Guide on How to Grill Anything, Learn Perfect Grilling Techniques and Become a Grillmaster

Descrierea CIP a Bibliotecii Naţionale a României
J.M. EDISON
    GRILL AND BARBECUE. The Ultimate Guide on How to Grill Anything, Learn Perfect Grilling Techniques and Become a Grillmaster / J.M. Edison – Bucharest: Editura My Ebook, 2021
    ISBN

J.M. EDISON

GRILL AND BARBECUE

**The Ultimate Guide on How to Grill Anything,
Learn Perfect Grilling Techniques
and Become a Grillmaster**

My Ebook Publishing House
Bucharest, 2021

CONTENTS

The Basics Of Grilling 7

Building The Fire 11

Tips For Cooking The Food 16

Beyond The Basics - Direct And Indirect Methods Of

Grilling 20

Searing - The Secret To The Perfect Steak 23

Rubs - Enhancing The Flavor Of Your Meats 28

Appetizers On The Grill 30

The Basics Of Grilling

Grilling is just like any other kind of cooking, it is a learned art. Keep this in mind as you are learning. You are sure to have some failures. The major difference between grilling and cooking on the stove or in the oven is that grilling is a combination of the two.

You have direct heat from the gas burners or the charcoal and you have indirect heat that fills the grill when the lid is put down. Grills also have higher heat and less control over that heat. With your oven you can set the temperature precisely, but with a grill you either turn on or light the fire and the heat will just keep rising.

The average gas grill can reach temperatures of 500 degrees in a just a few minutes. This is why you can't throw the food on the grill and walk away until the timer goes off. You must remain ever attentive. Monitoring is the key. The high heat, both direct and indirect is the basis of grilling.

You want to use this high heat to cook the food quickly, but, because foods will cook fast on a grill, you will have to turn them to get them to cook evenly and without burning. Although, if you turn the food too often you will just slow the process of cooking and this can lead to food that is tough and dry. The trick is to turn only when necessary. To check when the food is ready to be turned you will need to get down low, by the edge of the grill, being careful not to burn yourself, and lift up the corner of the meat. When the lines from the grills cooking grate start to turn black it's time to turn the food.

Knowing when to turn and when your food is cooked is the whole skill of successful grilling. The rest is just recipes and tricks. This skill however is also the hardest thing to teach, especially in a book. Ideally a steak should be turned only once. If you are cooking a thick cut of meat (over 1-1/2 inches) you may need to turn it three times to ensure it is cooked through to the center.

As a beginning grill master you should start simple. Thinner cuts of steaks, pork chops and burgers under 3/4 inches will let you get the "hang" of grilling and still get your food properly cooked. After you become experienced with these thinner cuts you can move on to more difficult foods.

Here are some useful tips for the beginning griller:

Tip 1: Keep your grill clean. A clean grill will give you better tasting food and is less likely to cause your food to stick to the grate.

Tip 2: Applying cooking oil or spray to the grill before it is lit will keep low fat meats and other foods from sticking.

Tip 3: Allow for plenty of time. You don't want to rush your grilling or keep your family or guests waiting.

Tip 4: Don't leave your grilling unattended for any length of time. A flare-up can occur at anytime and leave you with burnt food if you are not there to attend to it.

Tip 5: Flare-ups are caused by grease and heat. Trimming excess fat from the meat and moving the meat to a different area of the grill when turning is the best way to control flare-ups. Do not use a spray bottle of water to control a flare-up.

Tip 6: Don't add sugary or oily sauces or marinades to meat on the grill. This will just cause burning.

Tip 7: Apply spices or marinades to your food at least one hour before grilling. If using barbecue sauce, you should soak the food overnight. This will assure that the flavor gets into the food.

Tip 8: Using the proper tools is important. A fork should never be used for grilling. A long set of tongs is the best for turning steaks, chicken and other cuts of meat. A long handled spatula is best for burgers.

Building The Fire

Before you can become a grill master you will need to know how to properly build a fire. The fire is the beginning of the grilling process. Without a proper fire, you can not expect to be a real grill master. Even if you use a gas grill it is an important skill that will make you a better griller.

Building your charcoal fire is more than just opening up the bag, dumping in the charcoal, dousing them with lighter fluid and throwing on a match, although that is how many people do it. Then after 15-20 minutes they shake the grill to settle the coals and go to grilling. Do it this way and you will probably end up with burned burgers or raw chicken, but sometimes you might get lucky and your food will turn out okay. Wouldn't it be better to know that you will get good food every time?

The key to good grilling is to have an even fire. The only time you should have any variation in heat is when you plan for it. If you just dump your coals in randomly you will have hot and cool spots. If you evenly distribute the coals you can minimize any variation and get good, even grilling. This is very important when you are cooking a large amount of food on the grill.

The number of charcoal briquettes you use will depend on the size of your gill, the amount of food you will be cooking, weather conditions and cooking time.

As a general rule of thumb, plan on using about 30 briquettes to cook 1 pound of meat. A standard five-pound bag contains 75 to 90 briquettes. You want to make sure that you have enough briquettes to cover the grills pan in a single layer and extending out about 2" beyond the area of the food on the grill. The first step is to place the briquettes in the grills pan to determine the quantity and then stack them up in a rough pyramid shape to light. Soak the briquettes with approximately 1/2 cup of lighter fluid, and let set for a few minutes before lighting.

After the coals have begun to burn and ash starts to form, you will need to arrange them with long handled tongs into a single layer.

Once you have mastered even heating its time to step up to the professional level. A Pro likes to have a controlled temperature variation, a hot area and a not so hot area. In grilling this is called a two level fire. If you have a dual burner gas grill just set one burner on high and the other on medium. The advantage to this is that you will have one area to sear foods and another area to cook them through.

For a charcoal grill you will want to set up half of your fire grate in a single layer of coals and the other half in two or three layers of coals. This will give you the hot and medium areas to do your cooking. This method is also good if you are cooking different types of foods at the same time.

For instance if you were grilling fajitas, you would sear the steak over the high heat and cook the peppers over the lower heat. After you have mastered the two level fire you will certainly see the advantage of this method.

The other type of fire you need to learn how to build is the indirect fire. The simplest form of this of this fire is to put all the coals on one side of the grill and no coals on the other side. For a gas grill this is equivalent to turning the burner on one side on and leaving the other off. With a charcoal grill you can do much more than this. The ring of fire is an excellent strategy for an indirect fire if you are using the kettle style of grill. To build this type of fire, after you have hot coals, push the coals to the outside of the coal grate leaving the middle empty. This method gives you an even heat around the entire grill and a good indirect cooking space.

When building an indirect fire one of the most common problems is having the fire on just one side of the grill. If you are using a gas grill there isn't a lot you can do to avoid this. The problem with this is that the heat will be uneven and one side of the food you are cooking will get more heat than the other. This will require you to turn the food often to have it cook evenly. When you use a charcoal grill you can build the fire everywhere except under the food you are cooking and this gives you a more even heat.

Another thing to consider when building a fire is using hardwood. Using slow burning wood chips will add a smoky flavor to your food. If you are going to add wood chips to your fire then you will want to have a place to do that. For a gas grill you can use a firebox or wrap the moistened wood chips in foil. For a charcoal fire you will just need to leave a small area of the coal grate with just a coals. This makes a good place to put wood chips and they will smoke but not burn away quickly.

Tips For Cooking The Food

Whether you are using a charcoal grill or a gas grill, there are certain tips you need to know that will make you a better grill master. Below we have provided you with these tips. Follow them and you will be forever known by your family and friends as the "grillmaster"

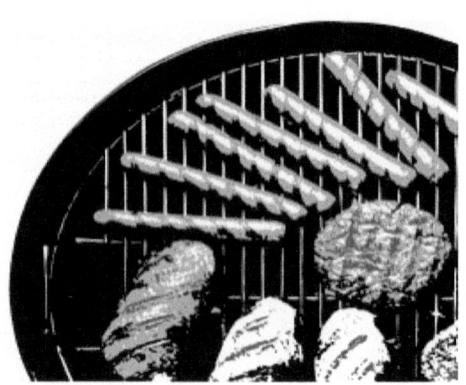

The addition of wood chips and chunks to your coals can add awesome flavor to your food. You should soak mesquite, alder, hickory and pecan chips for one hour before scattering over the hot coals.

Soak wood skewers in water for an hour before use. They are best used for foods that can be cooked quickly, like vegetables and fruits.

Use flat metal skewers when cooking meat kabobs. Round skewers will let the food turn and will not provide even cooking.

You should follow the recipes cooking times carefully, and make sure you cover the grill if the recipe calls for it.

When using sauces containing sugar and fat, apply them only during the last 10 minutes of cooking, unless the recipe instructions are different, or you will cause flareups and the food may burn.

Weather can affect grilling times and so can the length of time the food is being cooked. Here are some rules for maintaining cooking temperature:

➢ To lower the cooking temperature, you can raise the cooking grate, spread the coals farther apart, or adjust the vents on the grills pan to halfway closed.

➢ If you need to raise the temperature, you can lower the cooking grate, tap ash from the coals, move the coals closer together, or adjust the vents so that they are opened further. You can also add more charcoal to the outer edges of the hot coals.

➤ When the weather is cold, you will need to use more briquettes to achieve an ideal cooking temperature. Grilling will also take longer. Wind will tend to make the fire hotter and on a humid day, the coals will burn slower.

➤ The thickness and the temperature of the food when it is placed on the grill will affect it's cooking time. The colder and thicker the food, the longer it will take to cook.

➤ The closer the cooking grate is to the coals, the quicker the food will cook.

➤ Fires using hardwood will burn hotter than charcoal briquettes.

➤ Using a thermometer is the most reliable way to test when your food is done.

➤ Always follow the recipes instructions for testing doneness.

➤ Moving the food around on the grill will give you the most even cooking results, but don't turn the food to often or use a fork to move the food. Using a fork will release juices that you want in the food. Use a set of tongs or a spatula to move the food.

Beyond The Basics
Direct And Indirect Methods Of Grilling

When grilling you can use two different methods to cook, they are direct and indirect heat. For direct heat cooking, food is placed on the cooking rack directly over the hot coals or fire. The indirect method is used for more delicate foods and for larger cuts of meat that need longer cooking times, such as when you're barbecuing a thick roast.

The grill will always be kept covered when cooking with indirect heat.

Direct heat cooking is uncomplicated. Learning the temperature of the coals is the only real skill. If you are using a gas grill, you just need to set the heat settings at the proper level. The coals are ready when 3/4 of them are gray and coated with ash. You can check the temperature of a charcoal grill by very carefully holding your hand just above the grilling surface and counting the number of seconds it takes before the heat becomes uncomfortable enough for you to pull your hand away.

5 seconds equals Low Heat

4 seconds equals Medium Heat

3 seconds equals Medium-High Heat

2 seconds equals High Heat

You can use the following descriptions to check cooking temperature by observing the coals:

When the ash coating thickens and a red glow is just visible this would equal a low heat.

When the coals are covered with light gray ash this would equal a medium heat.

When the coals have a red glow visible through the ash coating this would equal a high heat.

The proper method for indirect heat cooking on a charcoal grill is to place an equal number of charcoal briquettes on each side of the grill pan and leaving a space in the center, light the briquettes and wait until they are at cooking temperature. When you are ready to start cooking, place a drip pan between the coals and add 1/2" of water to the pan. Place your food over the drip pan and then cover the grill. You will need to add 5 or 6 briquettes to each side of the pan as needed to maintain even heat. As a general rule, briquettes should be added every 45 minutes.

For indirect heat cooking on a dual burner gas grill, set the drip pan on the lava rocks on one side of the grill and add water to 1/2". Preheat the other burner on high for 5-10 minutes. Turn the temperature down to medium, then put the food on the rack over the drip pan and cover the grill.

For indirect heat cooking on a single burner gas grill, preheat the grill on high for 5-10 minutes. Turn the temperature down to low, and place a large foil baking pan on the rack. You can also line half of the cooking rack with a double thickness of heavy duty foil. Place food in the pan or on the foil, cover and cook.

Searing - The Secret To The Perfect Steak

Let me start out this section by saying that, for me, the perfect steak is medium rare. To cook a steak to well done is an unforgivable sin. That being said, if you want your steak well done, then don't use the searing method. If you do, you will end up with a steak that is charred and dry. Now that I have expressed my opinion on the perfect steak, let's get to the method.

To begin with, searing is not just for steaks. The best way to grill a great prime rib is to start it out at a high temperature and sear the surface and then lower the temperature to finish cooking it. Other meats as well, such as chicken, pork chops and roast will benefit from searing. The process of searing is essentially "browning" the meat, which gives it a delicious flavor and a little bit of a crusty surface. If your steak isn't browned it just isn't right.

What you want when you sear is to add that flavor and still end up with a juicy piece of meat. How can you get your meat seared just right? The first thing to know about searing is not to be apprehensive. Just because the meat has started to turn brown doesn't mean that it's time to turn it . You want the meat to have a dark brown color before turning, not just a golden color. This browning is what gives the steak the flavor you are looking for.

To get a good sear, there are steps that need to be taken before lighting the grill. You need to have a good clean grilling surface in order to have even contact between the metal and the meat. If you are using fatty cuts of meat you don't need to oil the grate, but if you do need to oil the grate, you want to use sunflower, canola or safflower oils because these oils will not break down at high temperatures like olive oil or lard. When oil breaks down it causes smoke and will leave an unpleasant taste to your meat.

The next thing is to make sure the surface of the meat is dry. If you use a marinade, make sure all the marinade is dripped off the meat before placing on the grill.

Now that you have a dry piece of meat and a clean grill, you will need to preheat the grill. If you are using a gas grill you will need to set both of the grills main burners to high and close the grill cover. You will want to let the grill get as hot as you can get it. If you know your grill you will know how long this takes. If you are a beginner about 10-15 minutes should do it.

If you are using a charcoal grill, you will need to build a two layer fire. This, as covered in a previous chapter requires that you build a two layer fire on one side of the grill and a single layer on the other. You will then sear the meat on one side of the grill and cook it the rest of the way on the other. Charcoal fires are ideal for searing because you get a more intense heat. You can tell when the charcoal fire is hot enough to sear by the hand test. You will not be able to hold your hand over the searing fire. For the finishing fire you want it at about medium-high heat (you can hold your hand over it for a count of three).

The grill is now ready for searing. Have everything you need close by because you will have to move fast. This is especially true for the gas grill. The grill has stored up as much heat as it can by now and you will want to keep as much of that heat inside the grill as possible. You will now need to lift the lid and get the meat on the grill as fast as you can and then re-close the lid.

If you are a beginner you are going to turn the meat after one minute. As you gain experience you can adjust this time so that you get the perfect browning. Your aim is to get a nice dark brown color to the meat without lifting the grills lid to check it. When turning the meat you want to act fast, as before, and position the meat as you turn it so that it is on a previously unused part of the grill. Sear this side for 1 minute and then open the grill. On a gas grill turn the heat down to medium-high and finish cooking, on the charcoal grill you will want to move the meat to the side with the single layer fire to finish. When you move the meat turn it the opposite way so that you get a criss cross grilling pattern on the meat.

If you are searing a roast or prime rib, you will need to move the meat to an indirect fire to finish it off.

After your meat has reached the desired doneness, remove it from the grill and let it sit for about five minutes before serving. This will let the juices in the meat return to the surface.

Just as with the other methods of grilling, searing will take some practice. If you find that the meat has been overcooked you will need to adjust accordingly. If you didn't get the dark brown sear that we are looking for, you will need to increase the time you sear a little bit. No two grills are the same and weather can also effect cooking times. Experience and patience is the key to getting the perfect sear and the perfect steak.

Rubs - Enhancing The Flavor Of Your Meats

You can use spices and seasonings to add flavor to your and color to your grilled foods. There are two different kinds of rubs, dry and wet. Dry rubs are made of spices and herbs which you can sprinkle on the meat or rub into the meat. Wet rubs have a liquid base, which is usually an oil, and is used to to coat the meats surface.

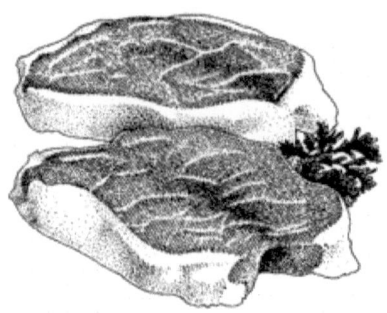

How you use rubs is a matter of personal taste. A good rub should add flavor and color to the food but not overwhelm the natural flavor of the food that you are using the rub on. Most dry rubs contain paprika, cayenne pepper and chili powder. You don't want to use to much cayenne pepper and make the meat so hot that you don't want to eat it. You should use a combination of strong and mild spices to add color and compliment the flavor of the food. There are many recipes and ready prepared rubs. The rub you use is really just your personal preference.

To get rubs to stay on the meat you need the meats natural moisture. To properly apply a rub you should work the rub into the meat evenly. If you are applying the rub to chicken or other poultry you should try to get the rub underneath the skin. The skin will block the flavor, so if you don't get it underneath, you won't be flavoring the meat.

The advantage of using a wet rub is that it will stay on the meat better. When using rubs on foods that are naturally dry or meats such as chicken with the skin on, you should use a wet rub. A wet rub will help keep meat from drying out and helps keep the meats natural juices inside. Using rubs with oil in them can help keep the food from sticking to your grill. Wet rubs should be about as thick as paste, so that they will stay on the food better.

You should always apply rubs at least an hour before you plan to grill. For chicken and roasts you should apply the rub the night before. You want the rubs to combine with the foods natural juices and penetrate the meat.

Appetizers On The Grill

Do you think that being the person in charge of the grill is a lonely and thankless job? You can make the grill the center of attention at your next gathering by making appetizers on the grill. Just about any hot appetizer can be prepared on the grill and it is much easier then you may think.

You can prepare tasty appetizers such as mini pizzas, mini tacos, buffalo wings and potato skins on the grill and they will be tastier than if you prepared them in your oven. The main difference between cooking appetizers on the grill and cooking them in the oven is that a grill will have a much more intense heat, even if you are using the indirect method. But if you coat the cooking surface with oil, use indirect heat and the upper rack and keep a close eye on your food you will be successful.

A tool that can be very useful when making appetizers is the grill topper. You can find grill toppers at hardware and department stores and it will be a good investment. You can use it as a tray and transfer everything to the preheated grill at once. When the food is cooked, just remove the grill topper and serve..

The trick to making the best appetizers for your gathering is to do as much of the preparation as possible in advance. You can prepare most of them a day in advance The mini pizzas, potato skins and buffalo wings can be already to cook and will just require a little heating on the grill to be ready to eat. The grill will heat them up fast too, so you won't need to stay around the grill to long.

You will want to match up the appetizers to the meal. If you are preparing steak a great appetizer is the potato skins. If you are making a Mexican meal try grilling up some beef strips and vegetables for fajitas as an appetizer. Another great appetizer that goes with almost anything is beef or chicken kabobs. They are easy to make if you prepare them the night before. My favorite is to use a good cut of roast and cut the meat into 1 inch cubes. Throw the cubes in a dish with thousand island dressing and let soak overnight. The next day cut up red and green peppers, mushrooms and sweet onion and alternate them on square metal skewers. They will cook in a few minutes and be ready for your guests.

If you plan on making appetizers and you use a charcoal grill, (My preference-I believe you get a much better flavor with a charcoal grill!) then I would suggest a two or three level fire. If you are making foods like the mini pizzas then you will be best served by the three level fire. You can heat the pizzas over the area of the grill with no coals. Other foods can be prepared at the same time over the other areas of the grill and when you are ready to make the main course you just need to add some coals.

Printed by Libri Plureos GmbH in Hamburg,
Germany